THE
GET IT
Together
PLANNER

◆ THIS PLANNER BELONGS TO ◆

_____

Ink &
Willow

THE GET IT TOGETHER PLANNER

Hardcover ISBN 978-0-593-19292-4

Design by Laura Palese and Jessie Kaye; Cover credit: Shutterstock Image (marble) by Crazy Lady; Creative Market "Cosmic Voyage Watercolor" gold foil by Veris Studio

Published in the United States by WaterBrook, an imprint of Random House, a division of Penguin Random House LLC, New York.

Ink & Willow and its colophon are trademarks of Penguin Random House LLC.

Printed in Thailand

2021—First Edition

10 9 8 7 6 5 4 3 2 1

SPECIAL SALES

Most WaterBrook and Ink & Willow books are available at special quantity discounts when purchased in bulk by corporations, organizations, and special-interest groups. Custom imprinting or excerpting can also be done to fit special needs. For information, please e-mail specialmarketscms@penguinrandomhouse.com.

LET'S GET IT TOGETHER!

*"The only thing worse than being blind is having sight
and no vision."* –HELEN KELLER

*If you're like many of us, you constantly feel the need to be more organized and productive.
But how do you even know where to begin when you're pulled in so many directions?*

Experts tell us the first step toward getting it together is to write down your vision. And here
in your new *Get It Together Planner*, you will find not only the space to record your vision but
also the tools you need to track your progress toward each of your intended goals.

As you plot out your daily activities and state your intentions for each week, it's important
to do all you can to ensure your plans are in alignment with God's purposes for you. Proverbs
16:9 reminds us, "In their hearts humans plan their course, but the Lord establishes their
steps." Sure, grocery lists and reading plans need your attention, but so does your soul. In the
pages that follow, you'll find reminders to engage your spiritual disciplines while developing
the tools you need to maximize your productivity.

HOW TO USE THIS PLANNER

*Your journey to productivity begins with the vision. On the first pages, use the space to describe
your ideal life. Whether it's writing in your own words, sketching with your pencil, or cutting and
pasting images from magazines, this space is designed to propel you forward and remind you of
what's important when setbacks and hurdles arise.*

Since this planner is designed to be your guide any time of year, it's undated, so you'll want to
write out the dates, using the yearly calendar guides on pages 4–5 and the stickers in the back
of the book.

At the beginning of each month, you'll see a motivational word designed to help inspire
your reflections, and lined spaces to set your intentions for each area of your life: physical
health, emotional well-being, family, relationships, spiritual growth, work/vocation, finances,
and creativity. You'll see a budget tracker and meal planner to help you develop discipline
around saving money and eating well. (Let's face it, we all need help in those areas.) At the end
of each month, you'll have a chance to celebrate your triumphs or lament the frustrations in
meeting those goals.

And every week, you'll find the practical tools to help you, one day at a time: to-do lists,
habit trackers, weekly priorities (high and low), prompts to record what you're thankful for,
and affirming messages from Scripture and voices to motivate you each step of the way.

At last, here is a planner to help you get it all together, reminding you that indeed, you can
do all things through Christ who strengthens you.

Yearly Calendars

2021

January
```
S  M  T  W  T  F  S
            1  2
3  4  5  6  7  8  9
10 11 12 13 14 15 16
17 18 19 20 21 22 23
24 25 26 27 28 29 30
31
```

February
```
S  M  T  W  T  F  S
   1  2  3  4  5  6
7  8  9 10 11 12 13
14 15 16 17 18 19 20
21 22 23 24 25 26 27
28
```

March
```
S  M  T  W  T  F  S
   1  2  3  4  5  6
7  8  9 10 11 12 13
14 15 16 17 18 19 20
21 22 23 24 25 26 27
28 29 30 31
```

April
```
S  M  T  W  T  F  S
            1  2  3
4  5  6  7  8  9 10
11 12 13 14 15 16 17
18 19 20 21 22 23 24
25 26 27 28 29 30
```

May
```
S  M  T  W  T  F  S
                  1
2  3  4  5  6  7  8
9 10 11 12 13 14 15
16 17 18 19 20 21 22
23 24 25 26 27 28 29
30 31
```

June
```
S  M  T  W  T  F  S
      1  2  3  4  5
6  7  8  9 10 11 12
13 14 15 16 17 18 19
20 21 22 23 24 25 26
27 28 29 30
```

July
```
S  M  T  W  T  F  S
            1  2  3
4  5  6  7  8  9 10
11 12 13 14 15 16 17
18 19 20 21 22 23 24
25 26 27 28 29 30 31
```

August
```
S  M  T  W  T  F  S
1  2  3  4  5  6  7
8  9 10 11 12 13 14
15 16 17 18 19 20 21
22 23 24 25 26 27 28
29 30 31
```

September
```
S  M  T  W  T  F  S
      1  2  3  4
5  6  7  8  9 10 11
12 13 14 15 16 17 18
19 20 21 22 23 24 25
26 27 28 29 30
```

October
```
S  M  T  W  T  F  S
               1  2
3  4  5  6  7  8  9
10 11 12 13 14 15 16
17 18 19 20 21 22 23
24 25 26 27 28 29 30
31
```

November
```
S  M  T  W  T  F  S
   1  2  3  4  5  6
7  8  9 10 11 12 13
14 15 16 17 18 19 20
21 22 23 24 25 26 27
28 29 30
```

December
```
S  M  T  W  T  F  S
         1  2  3  4
5  6  7  8  9 10 11
12 13 14 15 16 17 18
19 20 21 22 23 24 25
26 27 28 29 30 31
```

2022

January
```
S  M  T  W  T  F  S
                  1
2  3  4  5  6  7  8
9 10 11 12 13 14 15
16 17 18 19 20 21 22
23 24 25 26 27 28 29
30 31
```

February
```
S  M  T  W  T  F  S
      1  2  3  4  5
6  7  8  9 10 11 12
13 14 15 16 17 18 19
20 21 22 23 24 25 26
27 28
```

March
```
S  M  T  W  T  F  S
      1  2  3  4  5
6  7  8  9 10 11 12
13 14 15 16 17 18 19
20 21 22 23 24 25 26
27 28 29 30 31
```

April
```
S  M  T  W  T  F  S
               1  2
3  4  5  6  7  8  9
10 11 12 13 14 15 16
17 18 19 20 21 22 23
24 25 26 27 28 29 30
```

May
```
S  M  T  W  T  F  S
1  2  3  4  5  6  7
8  9 10 11 12 13 14
15 16 17 18 19 20 21
22 23 24 25 26 27 28
29 30 31
```

June
```
S  M  T  W  T  F  S
         1  2  3  4
5  6  7  8  9 10 11
12 13 14 15 16 17 18
19 20 21 22 23 24 25
26 27 28 29 30
```

July
```
S  M  T  W  T  F  S
            1  2
3  4  5  6  7  8  9
10 11 12 13 14 15 16
17 18 19 20 21 22 23
24 25 26 27 28 29 30
31
```

August
```
S  M  T  W  T  F  S
   1  2  3  4  5  6
7  8  9 10 11 12 13
14 15 16 17 18 19 20
21 22 23 24 25 26 27
28 29 30 31
```

September
```
S  M  T  W  T  F  S
         1  2  3
4  5  6  7  8  9 10
11 12 13 14 15 16 17
18 19 20 21 22 23 24
25 26 27 28 29 30
```

October
```
S  M  T  W  T  F  S
                  1
2  3  4  5  6  7  8
9 10 11 12 13 14 15
16 17 18 19 20 21 22
23 24 25 26 27 28 29
30 31
```

November
```
S  M  T  W  T  F  S
      1  2  3  4  5
6  7  8  9 10 11 12
13 14 15 16 17 18 19
20 21 22 23 24 25 26
27 28 29 30
```

December
```
S  M  T  W  T  F  S
            1  2  3
4  5  6  7  8  9 10
11 12 13 14 15 16 17
18 19 20 21 22 23 24
25 26 27 28 29 30 31
```

2023

January
```
S  M  T  W  T  F  S
1  2  3  4  5  6  7
8  9 10 11 12 13 14
15 16 17 18 19 20 21
22 23 24 25 26 27 28
29 30 31
```

February
```
S  M  T  W  T  F  S
         1  2  3  4
5  6  7  8  9 10 11
12 13 14 15 16 17 18
19 20 21 22 23 24 25
26 27 28
```

March
```
S  M  T  W  T  F  S
         1  2  3  4
5  6  7  8  9 10 11
12 13 14 15 16 17 18
19 20 21 22 23 24 25
26 27 28 29 30 31
```

April
```
S  M  T  W  T  F  S
                  1
2  3  4  5  6  7  8
9 10 11 12 13 14 15
16 17 18 19 20 21 22
23 24 25 26 27 28 29
30
```

May
```
S  M  T  W  T  F  S
   1  2  3  4  5  6
7  8  9 10 11 12 13
14 15 16 17 18 19 20
21 22 23 24 25 26 27
28 29 30 31
```

June
```
S  M  T  W  T  F  S
            1  2  3
4  5  6  7  8  9 10
11 12 13 14 15 16 17
18 19 20 21 22 23 24
25 26 27 28 29 30
```

July
```
S  M  T  W  T  F  S
                  1
2  3  4  5  6  7  8
9 10 11 12 13 14 15
16 17 18 19 20 21 22
23 24 25 26 27 28 29
30 31
```

August
```
S  M  T  W  T  F  S
      1  2  3  4  5
6  7  8  9 10 11 12
13 14 15 16 17 18 19
20 21 22 23 24 25 26
27 28 29 30 31
```

September
```
S  M  T  W  T  F  S
               1  2
3  4  5  6  7  8  9
10 11 12 13 14 15 16
17 18 19 20 21 22 23
24 25 26 27 28 29 30
```

October
```
S  M  T  W  T  F  S
1  2  3  4  5  6  7
8  9 10 11 12 13 14
15 16 17 18 19 20 21
22 23 24 25 26 27 28
29 30 31
```

November
```
S  M  T  W  T  F  S
         1  2  3  4
5  6  7  8  9 10 11
12 13 14 15 16 17 18
19 20 21 22 23 24 25
26 27 28 29 30
```

December
```
S  M  T  W  T  F  S
                  1  2
3  4  5  6  7  8  9
10 11 12 13 14 15 16
17 18 19 20 21 22 23
24 25 26 27 28 29 30
31
```

NOTES

2024

January
S	M	T	W	T	F	S
	1	2	3	4	5	6
7	8	9	10	11	12	13
14	15	16	17	18	19	20
21	22	23	24	25	26	27
28	29	30	31			

February
S	M	T	W	T	F	S
				1	2	3
4	5	6	7	8	9	10
11	12	13	14	15	16	17
18	19	20	21	22	23	24
25	26	27	28	29		

March
S	M	T	W	T	F	S
					1	2
3	4	5	6	7	8	9
10	11	12	13	14	15	16
17	18	19	20	21	22	23
24	25	26	27	28	29	30
31						

April
S	M	T	W	T	F	S
	1	2	3	4	5	6
7	8	9	10	11	12	13
14	15	16	17	18	19	20
21	22	23	24	25	26	27
28	29	30				

May
S	M	T	W	T	F	S
			1	2	3	4
5	6	7	8	9	10	11
12	13	14	15	16	17	18
19	20	21	22	23	24	25
26	27	28	29	30	31	

June
S	M	T	W	T	F	S
						1
2	3	4	5	6	7	8
9	10	11	12	13	14	15
16	17	18	19	20	21	22
23	24	25	26	27	28	29
30						

July
S	M	T	W	T	F	S
	1	2	3	4	5	6
7	8	9	10	11	12	13
14	15	16	17	18	19	20
21	22	23	24	25	26	27
28	29	30	31			

August
S	M	T	W	T	F	S
				1	2	3
4	5	6	7	8	9	10
11	12	13	14	15	16	17
18	19	20	21	22	23	24
25	26	27	28	29	30	31

September
S	M	T	W	T	F	S
1	2	3	4	5	6	7
8	9	10	11	12	13	14
15	16	17	18	19	20	21
22	23	24	25	26	27	28
29	30					

October
S	M	T	W	T	F	S
		1	2	3	4	5
6	7	8	9	10	11	12
13	14	15	16	17	18	19
20	21	22	23	24	25	26
27	28	29	30	31		

November
S	M	T	W	T	F	S
					1	2
3	4	5	6	7	8	9
10	11	12	13	14	15	16
17	18	19	20	21	22	23
24	25	26	27	28	29	30

December
S	M	T	W	T	F	S
1	2	3	4	5	6	7
8	9	10	11	12	13	14
15	16	17	18	19	20	21
22	23	24	25	26	27	28
29	30	31				

2025

January
S	M	T	W	T	F	S
			1	2	3	4
5	6	7	8	9	10	11
12	13	14	15	16	17	18
19	20	21	22	23	24	25
26	27	28	29	30	31	

February
S	M	T	W	T	F	S
						1
2	3	4	5	6	7	8
9	10	11	12	13	14	15
16	17	18	19	20	21	22
23	24	25	26	27	28	

March
S	M	T	W	T	F	S
						1
2	3	4	5	6	7	8
9	10	11	12	13	14	15
16	17	18	19	20	21	22
23	24	25	26	27	28	29
30	31					

April
S	M	T	W	T	F	S
		1	2	3	4	5
6	7	8	9	10	11	12
13	14	15	16	17	18	19
20	21	22	23	24	25	26
27	28	29	30			

May
S	M	T	W	T	F	S
				1	2	3
4	5	6	7	8	9	10
11	12	13	14	15	16	17
18	19	20	21	22	23	24
25	26	27	28	29	30	31

June
S	M	T	W	T	F	S
1	2	3	4	5	6	7
8	9	10	11	12	13	14
15	16	17	18	19	20	21
22	23	24	25	26	27	28
29	30					

July
S	M	T	W	T	F	S
		1	2	3	4	5
6	7	8	9	10	11	12
13	14	15	16	17	18	19
20	21	22	23	24	25	26
27	28	29	30	31		

August
S	M	T	W	T	F	S
					1	2
3	4	5	6	7	8	9
10	11	12	13	14	15	16
17	18	19	20	21	22	23
24	25	26	27	28	29	30
31						

September
S	M	T	W	T	F	S
	1	2	3	4	5	6
7	8	9	10	11	12	13
14	15	16	17	18	19	20
21	22	23	24	25	26	27
28	29	30				

October
S	M	T	W	T	F	S
			1	2	3	4
5	6	7	8	9	10	11
12	13	14	15	16	17	18
19	20	21	22	23	24	25
26	27	28	29	30	31	

November
S	M	T	W	T	F	S
						1
2	3	4	5	6	7	8
9	10	11	12	13	14	15
16	17	18	19	20	21	22
23	24	25	26	27	28	29
30						

December
S	M	T	W	T	F	S
	1	2	3	4	5	6
7	8	9	10	11	12	13
14	15	16	17	18	19	20
21	22	23	24	25	26	27
28	29	30	31			

2026

January
S	M	T	W	T	F	S
				1	2	3
4	5	6	7	8	9	10
11	12	13	14	15	16	17
18	19	20	21	22	23	24
25	26	27	28	29	30	31

February
S	M	T	W	T	F	S
1	2	3	4	5	6	7
8	9	10	11	12	13	14
15	16	17	18	19	20	21
22	23	24	25	26	27	28

March
S	M	T	W	T	F	S
1	2	3	4	5	6	7
8	9	10	11	12	13	14
15	16	17	18	19	20	21
22	23	24	25	26	27	28
29	30	31				

April
S	M	T	W	T	F	S
			1	2	3	4
5	6	7	8	9	10	11
12	13	14	15	16	17	18
19	20	21	22	23	24	25
26	27	28	29	30		

May
S	M	T	W	T	F	S
					1	2
3	4	5	6	7	8	9
10	11	12	13	14	15	16
17	18	19	20	21	22	23
24	25	26	27	28	29	30
31						

June
S	M	T	W	T	F	S
	1	2	3	4	5	6
7	8	9	10	11	12	13
14	15	16	17	18	19	20
21	22	23	24	25	26	27
28	29	30				

July
S	M	T	W	T	F	S
			1	2	3	4
5	6	7	8	9	10	11
12	13	14	15	16	17	18
19	20	21	22	23	24	25
26	27	28	29	30	31	

August
S	M	T	W	T	F	S
						1
2	3	4	5	6	7	8
9	10	11	12	13	14	15
16	17	18	19	20	21	22
23	24	25	26	27	28	29
30	31					

September
S	M	T	W	T	F	S
		1	2	3	4	5
6	7	8	9	10	11	12
13	14	15	16	17	18	19
20	21	22	23	24	25	26
27	28	29	30			

October
S	M	T	W	T	F	S
				1	2	3
4	5	6	7	8	9	10
11	12	13	14	15	16	17
18	19	20	21	22	23	24
25	26	27	28	29	30	31

November
S	M	T	W	T	F	S
1	2	3	4	5	6	7
8	9	10	11	12	13	14
15	16	17	18	19	20	21
22	23	24	25	26	27	28
29	30					

December
S	M	T	W	T	F	S
		1	2	3	4	5
6	7	8	9	10	11	12
13	14	15	16	17	18	19
20	21	22	23	24	25	26
27	28	29	30	31		

"Whatever your hand finds to do, do it with all your might."
-ECCLESIASTES 9:10

MY IDEAL
Life

MY *Vision Board*

Draw or paste pictures, words, or images to describe your ideal life.

Looking BACK

EVALUATING THE PAST YEAR

Physical Health
☆ ☆ ☆ ☆ ☆

Work Goals
☆ ☆ ☆ ☆ ☆

Relationship Goals
☆ ☆ ☆ ☆ ☆

Spiritual Growth
☆ ☆ ☆ ☆ ☆

Family Time
☆ ☆ ☆ ☆ ☆

Creativity
☆ ☆ ☆ ☆ ☆

Mental Health
☆ ☆ ☆ ☆ ☆

Financial Goals
☆ ☆ ☆ ☆ ☆

_____
☆ ☆ ☆ ☆ ☆

Would you give the areas above a 1-star review, a 5-star review, or something in between?

◆ WHAT WENT WELL LAST YEAR ◆

_____
_____
_____
_____
_____
_____
_____

◆ WHAT I AM LEAVING BEHIND FROM LAST YEAR ◆

_____
_____
_____
_____
_____
_____
_____

MONTH _____

YEAR 20 ____

SUN	MON	TUES	WED	THURS	FRI	SAT

GETTING IT TOGETHER THIS MONTH

Family _____

Work Goals _____

Wellness Goals _____

Relationship Health _____

Financial Goals _____

Emotional Health _____

Spiritual Growth _____

Special Projects _____

How will I live to the fullest this month?

MONTHLY *Budget Tracking*

MONTHLY EXPENSES			MONTHLY INCOME		
Category	Amount	Date Paid	Category	Amount	Date Received
Rent/Mortgage			Monthly Income		
Utility 1			Additional Earnings		
Utility 2			Gifts		
Utility 3			Savings from Previous Month		
Cell Phone					
Car/Transportation					
Savings					
Credit Card 1					
Credit Card 2					
TOTAL BILLS			TOTAL INCOME		

NOTES

_____

_____

_____

MONTHLY *Menu Planner*

MONTH 1

MEAL	MONDAY	TUESDAY	WEDNESDAY	THURSDAY	FRIDAY	SATURDAY	SUNDAY
Breakfast							
Lunch							
Dinner							

WEEK 1

WEEK 2

WEEK 3

WEEK 4

_____

WEEKLY
Priorities

HIGH

MEDIUM

DAILY
Habits

PRAYER
○ ○ ○ ○ ○ ○ ○

BIBLE
○ ○ ○ ○ ○ ○ ○

WATER
○ ○ ○ ○ ○ ○ ○

RECHARGE
○ ○ ○ ○ ○ ○ ○

_____
○ ○ ○ ○ ○ ○ ○

_____
○ ○ ○ ○ ○ ○ ○

_____
○ ○ ○ ○ ○ ○ ○

_____
○ ○ ○ ○ ○ ○ ○

MONDAY	TUESDAY	WEDNESDAY

This week I intend to:

I will focus on:

"For people this is impossible, but for God all things are possible." —MARK 10:27 (NCV)

THURSDAY	FRIDAY	SATURDAY

SUNDAY

I am thankful for:

Hurdles I will overcome:

Get- TO-DO LIST

◆

MEDIUM

◆

D A I L Y

Habits

PRAYER

○○○○○○○○

BIBLE

○○○○○○○○

WATER

○○○○○○○○

RECHARGE

○○○○○○○○

_____

○○○○○○○○

_____

○○○○○○○○

_____

○○○○○○○○

_____

○○○○○○○○

WEEK OF

_____

MONDAY	TUESDAY	WEDNESDAY

This week I intend to:

I will focus on:

"If you are always trying to be normal, you will never know how amazing you can be." **-MAYA ANGELOU**

THURSDAY	FRIDAY	SATURDAY

SUNDAY

I am thankful for:

Hurdles I will overcome:

Get-TO-DO LIST

WEEKLY
Priorities

HIGH

MEDIUM

DAILY
Habits

PRAYER
○ ○ ○ ○ ○ ○ ○

BIBLE
○ ○ ○ ○ ○ ○ ○

WATER
○ ○ ○ ○ ○ ○ ○

RECHARGE
○ ○ ○ ○ ○ ○ ○

○ ○ ○ ○ ○ ○

○ ○ ○ ○ ○ ○

○ ○ ○ ○ ○ ○

○ ○ ○ ○ ○ ○

WEEK OF

_____

MONDAY	TUESDAY	WEDNESDAY

This week I intend to:

I will focus on:

"Taste and see that the Lord is good. Oh, the joys of those who take refuge in him!" –PSALM 34:8

THURSDAY	FRIDAY	SATURDAY

SUNDAY

I am thankful for:

Hurdles I will overcome:

◆

WEEKLY
Priorities

HIGH

MEDIUM

◆

DAILY
Habits

PRAYER
◯ ◯ ◯ ◯ ◯ ◯ ◯

BIBLE
◯ ◯ ◯ ◯ ◯ ◯ ◯

WATER
◯ ◯ ◯ ◯ ◯ ◯ ◯

RECHARGE
◯ ◯ ◯ ◯ ◯ ◯ ◯

_____
◯ ◯ ◯ ◯ ◯ ◯ ◯

_____
◯ ◯ ◯ ◯ ◯ ◯ ◯

_____
◯ ◯ ◯ ◯ ◯ ◯ ◯

_____
◯ ◯ ◯ ◯ ◯ ◯ ◯

WEEK OF

_____

MONDAY	TUESDAY	WEDNESDAY

This week I intend to:

I will focus on:

"The chances you take, the people you meet, the people you love, the faith that you have. That's what's going to define you." –DENZEL WASHINGTON

THURSDAY	FRIDAY	SATURDAY

SUNDAY

I am thankful for:

Hurdles I will overcome:

◆
WEEKLY
Priorities

HIGH

MEDIUM

◆
DAILY
Habits

PRAYER
○ ○ ○ ○ ○ ○ ○

BIBLE
○ ○ ○ ○ ○ ○ ○

WATER
○ ○ ○ ○ ○ ○ ○

RECHARGE
○ ○ ○ ○ ○ ○ ○

○ ○ ○ ○ ○ ○ ○
_____

○ ○ ○ ○ ○ ○ ○
_____

○ ○ ○ ○ ○ ○ ○
_____

○ ○ ○ ○ ○ ○ ○

MONDAY	TUESDAY	WEDNESDAY

This week I intend to:

I will focus on:

"I am come that they might have life, and that they might have it more abundantly." –JOHN 10:10 (KJV)

THURSDAY	FRIDAY	SATURDAY

SUNDAY

I am thankful for:

Hurdles I will overcome:

Get-
TO-DO
LIST

Looking BACK

EVALUATING THE PAST MONTH

Physical Health
☆☆☆☆☆

Work Goals
☆☆☆☆☆

Relationship Goals
☆☆☆☆☆

Spiritual Growth
☆☆☆☆☆

Family Time
☆☆☆☆☆

Creativity
☆☆☆☆☆

Mental Health
☆☆☆☆☆

Financial Goals
☆☆☆☆☆

_____
☆☆☆☆☆

Would you give the areas above a 1-star review, a 5-star review, or something in between?

◆ WHAT WENT WELL THIS PAST MONTH ◆

_____
_____
_____
_____
_____
_____
_____

◆ WHAT DIDN'T GO WELL THIS PAST MONTH ◆

_____
_____
_____
_____
_____
_____
_____

MONTH _____

YEAR 20 ____

SUN	MON	TUES	WED	THURS	FRI	SAT

GETTING IT TOGETHER THIS MONTH

Family _____

Work Goals _____

Wellness Goals _____

Relationship Health _____

Financial Goals _____

Emotional Health _____

Spiritual Growth _____

Special Projects _____

How will I let myself breathe this month?

MONTHLY *Budget Tracking*

MONTHLY EXPENSES			MONTHLY INCOME		
Category	Amount	Date Paid	Category	Amount	Date Received
Rent/Mortgage			Monthly Income		
Utility 1			Additional Earnings		
Utility 2			Gifts		
Utility 3			Savings from Previous Month		
Cell Phone					
Car/Transportation					
Savings					
Credit Card 1					
Credit Card 2					
TOTAL BILLS			TOTAL INCOME		

NOTES _____

_____

_____

_____

_____

MONTHLY *Menu Planner*

MONTH 2

MEAL	MONDAY	TUESDAY	WEDNESDAY	THURSDAY	FRIDAY	SATURDAY	SUNDAY
Breakfast							
Lunch							
Dinner							

WEEK 1

MEAL	MONDAY	TUESDAY	WEDNESDAY	THURSDAY	FRIDAY	SATURDAY	SUNDAY
Breakfast							
Lunch							
Dinner							

WEEK 2

MEAL	MONDAY	TUESDAY	WEDNESDAY	THURSDAY	FRIDAY	SATURDAY	SUNDAY
Breakfast							
Lunch							
Dinner							

WEEK 3

MEAL	MONDAY	TUESDAY	WEDNESDAY	THURSDAY	FRIDAY	SATURDAY	SUNDAY
Breakfast							
Lunch							
Dinner							

WEEK 4

WEEKLY

Priorities

HIGH

MEDIUM

DAILY

Habits

PRAYER
○ ○ ○ ○ ○ ○ ○

BIBLE
○ ○ ○ ○ ○ ○ ○

WATER
○ ○ ○ ○ ○ ○ ○

RECHARGE
○ ○ ○ ○ ○ ○ ○

○ ○ ○ ○ ○ ○ ○

○ ○ ○ ○ ○ ○ ○

○ ○ ○ ○ ○ ○ ○

○ ○ ○ ○ ○ ○ ○

WEEK OF

MONDAY	TUESDAY	WEDNESDAY

This week I intend to:

I will focus on:

"Cast all your anxiety on him because he cares for you."
−1 PETER 5:7

Get-
TO-DO
LIST

THURSDAY	FRIDAY	SATURDAY

SUNDAY

I am thankful for:

Hurdles I will overcome:

WEEKLY
Priorities

HIGH

MEDIUM

DAILY
Habits

PRAYER
○ ○ ○ ○ ○ ○ ○

BIBLE
○ ○ ○ ○ ○ ○ ○

WATER
○ ○ ○ ○ ○ ○ ○

RECHARGE
○ ○ ○ ○ ○ ○ ○

○ ○ ○ ○ ○ ○ ○

○ ○ ○ ○ ○ ○ ○

○ ○ ○ ○ ○ ○ ○

○ ○ ○ ○ ○ ○ ○

WEEK OF

_____

MONDAY	TUESDAY	WEDNESDAY

This week I intend to:

I will focus on:

"God never made a promise that was too good to be true."

—DWIGHT L. MOODY

THURSDAY	FRIDAY	SATURDAY

SUNDAY

I am thankful for:

Hurdles I will overcome:

Get TO-DO LIST

WEEKLY
Priorities

HIGH

MEDIUM

DAILY
Habits

PRAYER
○ ○ ○ ○ ○ ○ ○

BIBLE
○ ○ ○ ○ ○ ○ ○

WATER
○ ○ ○ ○ ○ ○ ○

RECHARGE
○ ○ ○ ○ ○ ○ ○

○ ○ ○ ○ ○ ○ ○

○ ○ ○ ○ ○ ○ ○

○ ○ ○ ○ ○ ○ ○

○ ○ ○ ○ ○ ○ ○

WEEK OF

MONDAY	TUESDAY	WEDNESDAY

This week I intend to:

I will focus on:

"Cast your cares on the Lord and he will sustain you; he will never let the righteous be shaken." –PSALM 55:22

THURSDAY	FRIDAY	SATURDAY

SUNDAY

I am thankful for:

Hurdles I will overcome:

Get-
TO-DO
LIST

WEEKLY
Priorities

HIGH

MEDIUM

DAILY
Habits

PRAYER
○ ○ ○ ○ ○ ○ ○

BIBLE
○ ○ ○ ○ ○ ○ ○

WATER
○ ○ ○ ○ ○ ○ ○

RECHARGE
○ ○ ○ ○ ○ ○ ○

_____
○ ○ ○ ○ ○ ○ ○

_____
○ ○ ○ ○ ○ ○ ○

_____
○ ○ ○ ○ ○ ○ ○

_____
○ ○ ○ ○ ○ ○ ○

MONDAY	TUESDAY	WEDNESDAY

This week I intend to:

I will focus on:

"God's mercy does not waver or run out. He took care of our greatest need for salvation, so can He not also deal with our smaller needs of affliction?" –BLAIR LINNE

THURSDAY	FRIDAY	SATURDAY

SUNDAY

I am thankful for:

Hurdles I will overcome:

Get-TO-DO LIST

WEEKLY
Priorities

HIGH

MEDIUM

DAILY
Habits

PRAYER
○ ○ ○ ○ ○ ○ ○

BIBLE
○ ○ ○ ○ ○ ○ ○

WATER
○ ○ ○ ○ ○ ○ ○

RECHARGE
○ ○ ○ ○ ○ ○ ○

○ ○ ○ ○ ○ ○ ○

○ ○ ○ ○ ○ ○ ○

○ ○ ○ ○ ○ ○ ○

○ ○ ○ ○ ○ ○ ○

WEEK OF

_____

MONDAY	TUESDAY	WEDNESDAY

This week I intend to:

I will focus on:

"And my God will meet all your needs according to the riches of his glory in Christ Jesus." **–PHILIPPIANS 4:19**

THURSDAY	FRIDAY	SATURDAY

SUNDAY

I am thankful for:

Hurdles I will overcome:

Get-TO-DO LIST

Looking BACK

EVALUATING
THE
PAST MONTH

Physical Health
☆☆☆☆☆

Work Goals
☆☆☆☆☆

Relationship Goals
☆☆☆☆☆

Spiritual Growth
☆☆☆☆☆

Family Time
☆☆☆☆☆

Creativity
☆☆☆☆☆

Mental Health
☆☆☆☆☆

Financial Goals
☆☆☆☆☆

_____
☆☆☆☆☆

Would you give the areas above a 1-star review, a 5-star review, or something in between?

◆ WHAT WENT WELL THIS PAST MONTH ◆

_____
_____
_____
_____
_____
_____
_____
_____

◆ WHAT DIDN'T GO WELL THIS PAST MONTH ◆

_____
_____
_____
_____
_____
_____
_____

MONTH _____

YEAR 20 ____

SUN	MON	TUES	WED	THURS	FRI	SAT

GETTING IT TOGETHER THIS MONTH

Family _____

_____

_____

Wellness Goals _____

_____

_____

Emotional Health _____

_____

_____

Relationship Health _____

_____

_____

Spiritual Growth _____

_____

_____

Work Goals _____

_____

_____

Financial Goals _____

_____

_____

Special Projects _____

_____

_____

How will I remain consistent this month?

MONTHLY *Budget Tracking*

MONTHLY EXPENSES			MONTHLY INCOME		
Category	Amount	Date Paid	Category	Amount	Date Received
Rent/Mortgage			Monthly Income		
Utility 1			Additional Earnings		
Utility 2			Gifts		
Utility 3			Savings from Previous Month		
Cell Phone					
Car/Transportation					
Savings					
Credit Card 1					
Credit Card 2					
TOTAL BILLS			TOTAL INCOME		

NOTES

MEAL	MONDAY	TUESDAY	WEDNESDAY	THURSDAY	FRIDAY	SATURDAY	SUNDAY
Breakfast							
Lunch							
Dinner							

WEEK 1

MEAL	MONDAY	TUESDAY	WEDNESDAY	THURSDAY	FRIDAY	SATURDAY	SUNDAY
Breakfast							
Lunch							
Dinner							

WEEK 2

MEAL	MONDAY	TUESDAY	WEDNESDAY	THURSDAY	FRIDAY	SATURDAY	SUNDAY
Breakfast							
Lunch							
Dinner							

WEEK 3

MEAL	MONDAY	TUESDAY	WEDNESDAY	THURSDAY	FRIDAY	SATURDAY	SUNDAY
Breakfast							
Lunch							
Dinner							

WEEK 4

WEEKLY
Priorities

HIGH

MEDIUM

DAILY
Habits

PRAYER
○ ○ ○ ○ ○ ○ ○

BIBLE
○ ○ ○ ○ ○ ○ ○

WATER
○ ○ ○ ○ ○ ○ ○

RECHARGE
○ ○ ○ ○ ○ ○ ○

_____
○ ○ ○ ○ ○ ○ ○

_____
○ ○ ○ ○ ○ ○ ○

_____
○ ○ ○ ○ ○ ○ ○

_____
○ ○ ○ ○ ○ ○ ○

WEEK OF

_____

MONDAY	TUESDAY	WEDNESDAY

This week I intend to:

I will focus on:

"My purpose in writing is to encourage you and assure you that what you are experiencing is truly part of God's grace for you. Stand firm in this grace." **–1 PETER 5:12 (NLT)**

THURSDAY	FRIDAY	SATURDAY

SUNDAY

I am thankful for:

Hurdles I will overcome:

Get- TO-DO LIST

WEEKLY
Priorities

HIGH

MEDIUM

DAILY
Habits

PRAYER
◯ ◯ ◯ ◯ ◯ ◯ ◯

BIBLE
◯ ◯ ◯ ◯ ◯ ◯ ◯

WATER
◯ ◯ ◯ ◯ ◯ ◯ ◯

RECHARGE
◯ ◯ ◯ ◯ ◯ ◯ ◯

◯ ◯ ◯ ◯ ◯ ◯ ◯

◯ ◯ ◯ ◯ ◯ ◯ ◯

◯ ◯ ◯ ◯ ◯ ◯ ◯

◯ ◯ ◯ ◯ ◯ ◯ ◯

WEEK OF

MONDAY	TUESDAY	WEDNESDAY

This week I intend to:

I will focus on:

"Consistency is firmness of character. It's the ability to make mature, quality decisions time and again."
–REV. DR. A. R. BERNARD

THURSDAY	FRIDAY	SATURDAY

SUNDAY

I am thankful for:

Hurdles I will overcome:

WEEKLY
Priorities

HIGH

MEDIUM

DAILY
Habits

PRAYER
○ ○ ○ ○ ○ ○ ○

BIBLE
○ ○ ○ ○ ○ ○ ○

WATER
○ ○ ○ ○ ○ ○ ○

RECHARGE
○ ○ ○ ○ ○ ○ ○

○ ○ ○ ○ ○ ○ ○

○ ○ ○ ○ ○ ○ ○

○ ○ ○ ○ ○ ○ ○

○ ○ ○ ○ ○ ○ ○

WEEK OF

MONDAY	TUESDAY	WEDNESDAY

This week I intend to:

I will focus on:

"Trust in the Lord with all your heart, and lean not on your own understanding; In all your ways acknowledge Him, and He shall direct your paths." **–PROVERBS 3:5-6 (NKJV)**

Get-
TO-DO
LIST

THURSDAY	FRIDAY	SATURDAY

SUNDAY

I am thankful for:

Hurdles I will overcome:

WEEKLY
Priorities

HIGH

MEDIUM

DAILY
Habits

PRAYER
○○○○○○○

BIBLE
○○○○○○○

WATER
○○○○○○○

RECHARGE
○○○○○○○

○○○○○○○

○○○○○○○

○○○○○○○

○○○○○○○

MONDAY	TUESDAY	WEDNESDAY

This week I intend to:

I will focus on:

"Action may not always bring happiness; but there is no happiness without action." –BENJAMIN DISRAELI

THURSDAY	FRIDAY	SATURDAY

SUNDAY

I am thankful for:

Hurdles I will overcome:

WEEKLY
Priorities

HIGH

MEDIUM

DAILY
Habits

PRAYER
○○○○○○○

BIBLE
○○○○○○○

WATER
○○○○○○○

RECHARGE
○○○○○○○

○○○○○○○

○○○○○○○

○○○○○○○

○○○○○○○

WEEK OF
_____

MONDAY	TUESDAY	WEDNESDAY

This week I intend to:

I will focus on:

"Jesus Christ is the same yesterday, today, and forever."
—HEBREWS 13:8 (NLT)

THURSDAY	FRIDAY	SATURDAY

SUNDAY

I am thankful for:

Hurdles I will overcome:

Looking BACK

EVALUATING
THE
PAST MONTH

Physical Health	Work Goals	Relationship Goals
☆☆☆☆☆	☆☆☆☆☆	☆☆☆☆☆
Spiritual Growth	**Family Time**	**Creativity**
☆☆☆☆☆	☆☆☆☆☆	☆☆☆☆☆
Mental Health	**Financial Goals**	_____
☆☆☆☆☆	☆☆☆☆☆	☆☆☆☆☆

Would you give the areas above a 1-star review, a 5-star review, or something in between?

◆ WHAT WENT WELL THIS PAST MONTH ◆

_____

_____

_____

_____

_____

_____

_____

_____

◆ WHAT DIDN'T GO WELL THIS PAST MONTH ◆

_____

_____

_____

_____

_____

_____

_____

Dare to Dream

SUN	MON	TUES	WED	THURS	FRI	SAT

GETTING IT TOGETHER THIS MONTH

Family _____

_____

_____

Work Goals _____

_____

Wellness Goals _____

_____

Relationship Health _____

_____

Financial Goals _____

_____

Emotional Health _____

_____

Spiritual Growth _____

_____

Special Projects _____

_____

How will I dare to dream this month?

MONTHLY *Budget Tracking*

MONTHLY EXPENSES			MONTHLY INCOME		
Category	Amount	Date Paid	Category	Amount	Date Received
Rent/Mortgage			Monthly Income		
Utility 1			Additional Earnings		
Utility 2			Gifts		
Utility 3			Savings from Previous Month		
Cell Phone					
Car/Transportation					
Savings					
Credit Card 1					
Credit Card 2					
TOTAL BILLS			TOTAL INCOME		

NOTES _____

_____

_____

MEAL	MONDAY	TUESDAY	WEDNESDAY	THURSDAY	FRIDAY	SATURDAY	SUNDAY
Breakfast							
Lunch							
Dinner							

WEEK 1

MEAL	MONDAY	TUESDAY	WEDNESDAY	THURSDAY	FRIDAY	SATURDAY	SUNDAY
Breakfast							
Lunch							
Dinner							

WEEK 2

MEAL	MONDAY	TUESDAY	WEDNESDAY	THURSDAY	FRIDAY	SATURDAY	SUNDAY
Breakfast							
Lunch							
Dinner							

WEEK 3

MEAL	MONDAY	TUESDAY	WEDNESDAY	THURSDAY	FRIDAY	SATURDAY	SUNDAY
Breakfast							
Lunch							
Dinner							

WEEK 4

◆

W E E K L Y
Priorities

HIGH

MEDIUM

MONDAY	TUESDAY	WEDNESDAY

◆

D A I L Y
Habits

PRAYER
○ ○ ○ ○ ○ ○ ○

BIBLE
○ ○ ○ ○ ○ ○ ○

WATER
○ ○ ○ ○ ○ ○ ○

RECHARGE
○ ○ ○ ○ ○ ○ ○

○ ○ ○ ○ ○ ○ ○

○ ○ ○ ○ ○ ○ ○

○ ○ ○ ○ ○ ○ ○

○ ○ ○ ○ ○ ○ ○

This week I intend to:

I will focus on:

*"Write the vision
And make it plain on tablets,
That he may run who reads it."* –HABAKKUK 2:2 (NKJV)

THURSDAY	FRIDAY	SATURDAY

SUNDAY

I am thankful for:

Hurdles I will overcome:

WEEKLY
Priorities

HIGH

MEDIUM

DAILY
Habits

PRAYER
○ ○ ○ ○ ○ ○ ○

BIBLE
○ ○ ○ ○ ○ ○ ○

WATER
○ ○ ○ ○ ○ ○ ○

RECHARGE
○ ○ ○ ○ ○ ○ ○

○ ○ ○ ○ ○ ○ ○

○ ○ ○ ○ ○ ○ ○

○ ○ ○ ○ ○ ○ ○

○ ○ ○ ○ ○ ○ ○

MONDAY	TUESDAY	WEDNESDAY

This week I intend to:

I will focus on:

"I knew that if God loved me, then I could do wonderful things, I could try great things, learn anything, achieve anything." **–MAYA ANGELOU**

Get-
TO-DO
LIST

THURSDAY	FRIDAY	SATURDAY

SUNDAY

I am thankful for:

Hurdles I will overcome:

◆

WEEKLY

Priorities

HIGH

MEDIUM

◆

DAILY

Habits

PRAYER

◯ ◯ ◯ ◯ ◯ ◯ ◯

BIBLE

◯ ◯ ◯ ◯ ◯ ◯ ◯

WATER

◯ ◯ ◯ ◯ ◯ ◯ ◯

RECHARGE

◯ ◯ ◯ ◯ ◯ ◯ ◯

◯ ◯ ◯ ◯ ◯ ◯ ◯

◯ ◯ ◯ ◯ ◯ ◯ ◯

◯ ◯ ◯ ◯ ◯ ◯ ◯

◯ ◯ ◯ ◯ ◯ ◯ ◯

WEEK OF

_____

MONDAY	TUESDAY	WEDNESDAY

This week I intend to:

I will focus on:

"For I can do everything through Christ, who gives me strength." –PHILIPPIANS 4:13 (NLT)

THURSDAY	FRIDAY	SATURDAY

SUNDAY

I am thankful for:

Hurdles I will overcome:

◆

WEEKLY
Priorities

HIGH

MEDIUM

◆

DAILY
Habits

PRAYER
◯◯◯◯◯◯◯

BIBLE
◯◯◯◯◯◯◯

WATER
◯◯◯◯◯◯◯

RECHARGE
◯◯◯◯◯◯◯

_____
◯◯◯◯◯◯◯

_____
◯◯◯◯◯◯◯

_____
◯◯◯◯◯◯◯

_____
◯◯◯◯◯◯◯

WEEK OF

_____

MONDAY	TUESDAY	WEDNESDAY

This week I intend to:

I will focus on:

"When we get out of our own way and let the spirit of love and hope shine through, we are a better people."
—MICHAEL ERIC DYSON

THURSDAY	FRIDAY	SATURDAY

SUNDAY

I am thankful for:

Hurdles I will overcome:

◆

WEEKLY

Priorities

HIGH

MEDIUM

MONDAY	TUESDAY	WEDNESDAY

◆

DAILY

Habits

PRAYER

○ ○ ○ ○ ○ ○ ○

BIBLE

○ ○ ○ ○ ○ ○ ○

WATER

○ ○ ○ ○ ○ ○ ○

RECHARGE

○ ○ ○ ○ ○ ○ ○

_____
○ ○ ○ ○ ○ ○ ○

_____
○ ○ ○ ○ ○ ○ ○

_____
○ ○ ○ ○ ○ ○ ○

_____
○ ○ ○ ○ ○ ○ ○

This week I intend to:

I will focus on:

"Now to him who is able to do immeasurably more than all we ask or imagine, according to his power that is at work within us." –EPHESIANS 3:20

THURSDAY	FRIDAY	SATURDAY
		SUNDAY

I am thankful for:

Hurdles I will overcome:

Get-
TO-DO
LIST

Looking BACK

EVALUATING
THE
PAST MONTH

Physical Health
☆☆☆☆☆

Work Goals
☆☆☆☆☆

Relationship Goals
☆☆☆☆☆

Spiritual Growth
☆☆☆☆☆

Family Time
☆☆☆☆☆

Creativity
☆☆☆☆☆

Mental Health
☆☆☆☆☆

Financial Goals
☆☆☆☆☆

_____
☆☆☆☆☆

Would you give the areas above a 1-star review, a 5-star review, or something in between?

◆ WHAT WENT WELL THIS PAST MONTH ◆

_____
_____
_____
_____
_____
_____
_____

◆ WHAT DIDN'T GO WELL THIS PAST MONTH ◆

_____
_____
_____
_____
_____
_____
_____

MONTH _____

YEAR 20 ____

SUN	MON	TUES	WED	THURS	FRI	SAT

GETTING IT TOGETHER THIS MONTH

Family _____

Work Goals _____

Wellness Goals _____

Relationship Health _____

Financial Goals _____

Emotional Health _____

Spiritual Growth _____

Special Projects _____

How will I be decisive this month?

MONTHLY *Budget Tracking*

MONTHLY EXPENSES			MONTHLY INCOME		
Category	Amount	Date Paid	Category	Amount	Date Received
Rent/Mortgage			Monthly Income		
Utility 1			Additional Earnings		
Utility 2			Gifts		
Utility 3			Savings from Previous Month		
Cell Phone					
Car/Transportation					
Savings					
Credit Card 1					
Credit Card 2					
TOTAL BILLS			TOTAL INCOME		

NOTES

MEAL	MONDAY	TUESDAY	WEDNESDAY	THURSDAY	FRIDAY	SATURDAY	SUNDAY
Breakfast							
Lunch							
Dinner							

WEEK 1

MEAL	MONDAY	TUESDAY	WEDNESDAY	THURSDAY	FRIDAY	SATURDAY	SUNDAY
Breakfast							
Lunch							
Dinner							

WEEK 2

MEAL	MONDAY	TUESDAY	WEDNESDAY	THURSDAY	FRIDAY	SATURDAY	SUNDAY
Breakfast							
Lunch							
Dinner							

WEEK 3

MEAL	MONDAY	TUESDAY	WEDNESDAY	THURSDAY	FRIDAY	SATURDAY	SUNDAY
Breakfast							
Lunch							
Dinner							

WEEK 4

◆

WEEKLY

Priorities

HIGH

MEDIUM

◆

DAILY

Habits

PRAYER

○ ○ ○ ○ ○ ○ ○

BIBLE

○ ○ ○ ○ ○ ○ ○

WATER

○ ○ ○ ○ ○ ○ ○

RECHARGE

○ ○ ○ ○ ○ ○ ○

_____
○ ○ ○ ○ ○ ○ ○

_____
○ ○ ○ ○ ○ ○ ○

_____
○ ○ ○ ○ ○ ○ ○

_____
○ ○ ○ ○ ○ ○ ○

WEEK OF

_____

MONDAY	TUESDAY	WEDNESDAY

This week I intend to:

I will focus on:

"Discretion will watch over you,
Understanding and discernment will guard you."
PROVERBS 2:11 (AMP)

THURSDAY	FRIDAY	SATURDAY

SUNDAY

am thankful for:

Hurdles I will overcome:

Get-
TO-DO
LIST

◆

WEEKLY
Priorities

HIGH

MEDIUM

◆

DAILY
Habits

PRAYER

○○○○○○○

BIBLE

○○○○○○○

WATER

○○○○○○○

RECHARGE

○○○○○○○

_____

○○○○○○○

_____

○○○○○○○

_____

○○○○○○○

_____

○○○○○○○

WEEK OF

_____

MONDAY	TUESDAY	WEDNESDAY

This week I intend to:

I will focus on:

"We often can't see what God is doing in our lives, but God sees the whole picture and His plan for us clearly."
TONY DUNGY

THURSDAY	FRIDAY	SATURDAY

SUNDAY

am thankful for:

Hurdles I will overcome:

◆

WEEKLY
Priorities

HIGH

MEDIUM

◆

DAILY
Habits

PRAYER
○ ○ ○ ○ ○ ○ ○

BIBLE
○ ○ ○ ○ ○ ○ ○

WATER
○ ○ ○ ○ ○ ○ ○

RECHARGE
○ ○ ○ ○ ○ ○ ○

○ ○ ○ ○ ○ ○ ○

○ ○ ○ ○ ○ ○ ○

○ ○ ○ ○ ○ ○ ○

○ ○ ○ ○ ○ ○ ○

WEEK OF

_____

MONDAY	TUESDAY	WEDNESDAY

This week I intend to:

I will focus on:

'What, then, shall we say in response to these things? If God s for us, who can be against us?" —ROMANS 8:31

THURSDAY	FRIDAY	SATURDAY

SUNDAY

am thankful for:

Hurdles I will overcome:

Get- TO-DO LIST

WEEKLY

Priorities

HIGH

MEDIUM

DAILY

Habits

PRAYER
○ ○ ○ ○ ○ ○ ○

BIBLE
○ ○ ○ ○ ○ ○ ○

WATER
○ ○ ○ ○ ○ ○ ○

RECHARGE
○ ○ ○ ○ ○ ○ ○

○ ○ ○ ○ ○ ○ ○

○ ○ ○ ○ ○ ○ ○

○ ○ ○ ○ ○ ○ ○

○ ○ ○ ○ ○ ○ ○

MONDAY	TUESDAY	WEDNESDAY

This week I intend to:

I will focus on:

"The most difficult thing is the decision to act, the rest is merely tenacity." **-AMELIA EARHART**

THURSDAY	FRIDAY	SATURDAY

SUNDAY

Get-
TO-DO
LIST

I am thankful for:

Hurdles I will overcome:

◆

W E E K L Y

Priorities

HIGH

MEDIUM

◆

D A I L Y

Habits

PRAYER
○ ○ ○ ○ ○ ○ ○

BIBLE
○ ○ ○ ○ ○ ○ ○

WATER
○ ○ ○ ○ ○ ○ ○

RECHARGE
○ ○ ○ ○ ○ ○ ○

○ ○ ○ ○ ○ ○ ○

○ ○ ○ ○ ○ ○ ○

○ ○ ○ ○ ○ ○ ○

○ ○ ○ ○ ○ ○ ○

MONDAY	TUESDAY	WEDNESDAY

This week I intend to:

I will focus on:

"The Lord is my strength and song, And He has become my salvation; He is my God, and I will praise Him; My father's God, and I will exalt Him." -**EXODUS 15:2 (NKJV)**

THURSDAY	FRIDAY	SATURDAY

SUNDAY

I am thankful for:

Hurdles I will overcome:

Looking BACK

EVALUATING THE PAST MONTH

Physical Health
☆☆☆☆☆

Work Goals
☆☆☆☆☆

Relationship Goals
☆☆☆☆☆

Spiritual Growth
☆☆☆☆☆

Family Time
☆☆☆☆☆

Creativity
☆☆☆☆☆

Mental Health
☆☆☆☆☆

Financial Goals
☆☆☆☆☆

_____
☆☆☆☆☆

Would you give the areas above a 1-star review, a 5-star review, or something in between?

◆ WHAT WENT WELL THIS PAST MONTH ◆

_____

_____

_____

_____

_____

_____

_____

◆ WHAT DIDN'T GO WELL THIS PAST MONTH ◆

_____

_____

_____

_____

_____

_____

_____

MONTH _____

YEAR 20 ____

SUN	MON	TUES	WED	THURS	FRI	SAT

GETTING IT TOGETHER THIS MONTH

Family _____

_____

_____

Work Goals _____

_____

Wellness Goals _____

_____

_____

Relationship Health _____

_____

_____

Financial Goals _____

_____

_____

Emotional Health _____

_____

_____

Spiritual Growth _____

_____

_____

Special Projects _____

_____

_____

How will I practice discipline this month?

MONTHLY *Budget Tracking*

MONTHLY EXPENSES			MONTHLY INCOME		
Category	Amount	Date Paid	Category	Amount	Date Received
Rent/Mortgage			Monthly Income		
Utility 1			Additional Earnings		
Utility 2			Gifts		
Utility 3			Savings from Previous Month		
Cell Phone					
Car/Transportation					
Savings					
Credit Card 1					
Credit Card 2					
TOTAL BILLS			TOTAL INCOME		

NOTES _____

_____

_____

_____

_____

MEAL	MONDAY	TUESDAY	WEDNESDAY	THURSDAY	FRIDAY	SATURDAY	SUNDAY
Breakfast							
Lunch							
Dinner							

WEEK 1

MEAL	MONDAY	TUESDAY	WEDNESDAY	THURSDAY	FRIDAY	SATURDAY	SUNDAY
Breakfast							
Lunch							
Dinner							

WEEK 2

MEAL	MONDAY	TUESDAY	WEDNESDAY	THURSDAY	FRIDAY	SATURDAY	SUNDAY
Breakfast							
Lunch							
Dinner							

WEEK 3

MEAL	MONDAY	TUESDAY	WEDNESDAY	THURSDAY	FRIDAY	SATURDAY	SUNDAY
Breakfast							
Lunch							
Dinner							

WEEK 4

WEEKLY
Priorities

HIGH

MEDIUM

DAILY
Habits

PRAYER

○ ○ ○ ○ ○ ○ ○

BIBLE

○ ○ ○ ○ ○ ○ ○

WATER

○ ○ ○ ○ ○ ○ ○

RECHARGE

○ ○ ○ ○ ○ ○ ○

○ ○ ○ ○ ○ ○ ○

○ ○ ○ ○ ○ ○ ○

○ ○ ○ ○ ○ ○ ○

○ ○ ○ ○ ○ ○ ○

WEEK OF

MONDAY	TUESDAY	WEDNESDAY

This week I intend to:

I will focus on:

Get-TO-DO LIST

THURSDAY	FRIDAY	SATURDAY

SUNDAY

I am thankful for:

Hurdles I will overcome:

WEEKLY
Priorities

HIGH

MEDIUM

DAILY
Habits

PRAYER
○○○○○○○

BIBLE
○○○○○○○

WATER
○○○○○○○

RECHARGE
○○○○○○○

_____
○○○○○○○

_____
○○○○○○○

_____
○○○○○○○

_____
○○○○○○○

MONDAY	TUESDAY	WEDNESDAY

This week I intend to:

I will focus on:

"If you believe you can change—if you make it a habit—the change becomes real." **–CHARLES DUHIGG**

THURSDAY	FRIDAY	SATURDAY

SUNDAY

I am thankful for:

Hurdles I will overcome:

WEEKLY
Priorities

HIGH

MEDIUM

DAILY
Habits

PRAYER

◯◯◯◯◯◯◯

BIBLE

◯◯◯◯◯◯◯

WATER

◯◯◯◯◯◯◯

RECHARGE

◯◯◯◯◯◯◯

◯◯◯◯◯◯◯

◯◯◯◯◯◯◯

◯◯◯◯◯◯◯

◯◯◯◯◯◯◯

MONDAY	TUESDAY	WEDNESDAY

This week I intend to:

I will focus on:

"And we know that all things work together for good to those who love God, to those who are the called according to His purpose." –ROMANS 8:28 (NKJV)

THURSDAY	FRIDAY	SATURDAY
		SUNDAY

I am thankful for:

Hurdles I will overcome:

Get-
TO-DO
LIST

MEDIUM

◆

D A I L Y

Habits

PRAYER

○ ○ ○ ○ ○ ○ ○

BIBLE

○ ○ ○ ○ ○ ○ ○

WATER

○ ○ ○ ○ ○ ○ ○

RECHARGE

○ ○ ○ ○ ○ ○ ○

○ ○ ○ ○ ○ ○ ○

○ ○ ○ ○ ○ ○ ○

○ ○ ○ ○ ○ ○ ○

○ ○ ○ ○ ○ ○ ○

WEEK OF
_____

MONDAY	TUESDAY	WEDNESDAY

This week I intend to:

I will focus on:

"Be faithful in small things because it is in them that your strength lies." **–MOTHER TERESA**

THURSDAY	FRIDAY	SATURDAY

SUNDAY

I am thankful for:

Hurdles I will overcome:

WEEKLY
Priorities

HIGH

MEDIUM

◆
DAILY
Habits

PRAYER
○ ○ ○ ○ ○ ○ ○

BIBLE
○ ○ ○ ○ ○ ○ ○

WATER
○ ○ ○ ○ ○ ○ ○

RECHARGE
○ ○ ○ ○ ○ ○ ○

○ ○ ○ ○ ○ ○ ○

○ ○ ○ ○ ○ ○ ○

○ ○ ○ ○ ○ ○ ○

○ ○ ○ ○ ○ ○ ○

WEEK OF

_____

MONDAY	TUESDAY	WEDNESDAY

This week I intend to:

I will focus on:

"Stand your ground. Throw yourselves into the work of the Master, confident that nothing you do for him is a waste of time or effort." –1 CORINTHIANS 15:58 (MSG)

THURSDAY	FRIDAY	SATURDAY

SUNDAY

Get-TO-DO LIST

am thankful for:

Hurdles I will overcome:

Looking BACK

EVALUATING
THE
PAST MONTH

| Physical Health | Work Goals | Relationship Goals |
| ☆ ☆ ☆ ☆ ☆ | ☆ ☆ ☆ ☆ ☆ | ☆ ☆ ☆ ☆ ☆ |

| Spiritual Growth | Family Time | Creativity |
| ☆ ☆ ☆ ☆ ☆ | ☆ ☆ ☆ ☆ ☆ | ☆ ☆ ☆ ☆ ☆ |

| Mental Health | Financial Goals | _____ |
| ☆ ☆ ☆ ☆ ☆ | ☆ ☆ ☆ ☆ ☆ | ☆ ☆ ☆ ☆ ☆ |

Would you give the areas above a 1-star review, a 5-star review, or something in between?

◆ WHAT WENT WELL THIS PAST MONTH ◆

_____
_____
_____
_____
_____
_____
_____
_____
_____

◆ WHAT DIDN'T GO WELL THIS PAST MONTH ◆

_____
_____
_____
_____
_____
_____
_____
_____

Endurance

MONTH _____

YEAR 20 ____

SUN	MON	TUES	WED	THURS	FRI	SAT

GETTING IT TOGETHER THIS MONTH

Family _____

_____

_____

Wellness Goals _____

_____

_____

Emotional Health _____

_____

_____

Relationship Health _____

_____

_____

Spiritual Growth _____

_____

_____

Work Goals _____

_____

_____

Financial Goals _____

_____

_____

Special Projects _____

_____

_____

How will I improve my endurance this month?

MONTHLY *Budget Tracking*

MONTHLY EXPENSES			MONTHLY INCOME		
Category	Amount	Date Paid	Category	Amount	Date Received
Rent/Mortgage			Monthly Income		
Utility 1			Additional Earnings		
Utility 2			Gifts		
Utility 3			Savings from Previous Month		
Cell Phone					
Car/Transportation					
Savings					
Credit Card 1					
Credit Card 2					
TOTAL BILLS			TOTAL INCOME		

NOTES

MEAL	MONDAY	TUESDAY	WEDNESDAY	THURSDAY	FRIDAY	SATURDAY	SUNDAY
Breakfast							
Lunch							
Dinner							

WEEK 1

MEAL	MONDAY	TUESDAY	WEDNESDAY	THURSDAY	FRIDAY	SATURDAY	SUNDAY
Breakfast							
Lunch							
Dinner							

WEEK 2

MEAL	MONDAY	TUESDAY	WEDNESDAY	THURSDAY	FRIDAY	SATURDAY	SUNDAY
Breakfast							
Lunch							
Dinner							

WEEK 3

MEAL	MONDAY	TUESDAY	WEDNESDAY	THURSDAY	FRIDAY	SATURDAY	SUNDAY
Breakfast							
Lunch							
Dinner							

WEEK 4

WEEKLY
Priorities

HIGH

MEDIUM

DAILY
Habits

PRAYER
○ ○ ○ ○ ○ ○ ○

BIBLE
○ ○ ○ ○ ○ ○ ○

WATER
○ ○ ○ ○ ○ ○ ○

RECHARGE
○ ○ ○ ○ ○ ○ ○

○ ○ ○ ○ ○ ○ ○

○ ○ ○ ○ ○ ○ ○

○ ○ ○ ○ ○ ○ ○

○ ○ ○ ○ ○ ○ ○

MONDAY	TUESDAY	WEDNESDAY

This week I intend to:

I will focus on:

"If you can't fly, run. If you can't run, walk. If you can't walk, crawl, but by all means keep moving."
—DR. MARTIN LUTHER KING JR.

THURSDAY	FRIDAY	SATURDAY

SUNDAY

I am thankful for:

Hurdles I will overcome:

Get- TO-DO LIST

WEEKLY

Priorities

HIGH

MEDIUM

◆

DAILY

Habits

PRAYER

○○○○○○○

BIBLE

○○○○○○○

WATER

○○○○○○○

RECHARGE

○○○○○○○

○○○○○○○

○○○○○○○

○○○○○○○

○○○○○○○

WEEK OF

_____

MONDAY	TUESDAY	WEDNESDAY

This week I intend to:

I will focus on:

"Be brave. Be strong. Don't give up. Expect God to get here soon." –PSALM 31:24 (MSG)

THURSDAY	FRIDAY	SATURDAY

SUNDAY

am thankful for:

Hurdles I will overcome:

WEEKLY
Priorities

HIGH

MEDIUM

DAILY
Habits

PRAYER
○○○○○○○

BIBLE
○○○○○○○

WATER
○○○○○○○

RECHARGE
○○○○○○○

○○○○○○○

○○○○○○○

○○○○○○○

○○○○○○○

MONDAY	TUESDAY	WEDNESDAY

This week I intend to:

I will focus on:

"God never said that the journey would be easy, but He did say that the arrival would be worthwhile." –MAX LUCADO

THURSDAY	FRIDAY	SATURDAY

SUNDAY

am thankful for:

Hurdles I will overcome:

Get-TO-DO LIST

WEEKLY
Priorities

HIGH

MEDIUM

DAILY
Habits

PRAYER
○ ○ ○ ○ ○ ○ ○

BIBLE
○ ○ ○ ○ ○ ○ ○

WATER
○ ○ ○ ○ ○ ○ ○

RECHARGE
○ ○ ○ ○ ○ ○ ○

○ ○ ○ ○ ○ ○ ○

○ ○ ○ ○ ○ ○ ○

○ ○ ○ ○ ○ ○ ○

○ ○ ○ ○ ○ ○ ○

MONDAY	TUESDAY	WEDNESDAY

This week I intend to:

I will focus on:

"When you pass through the waters, I will be with you; and when you pass through the rivers, they will not sweep over you." —ISAIAH 43:2

Get-TO-DO LIST

THURSDAY	FRIDAY	SATURDAY

SUNDAY

I am thankful for:

Hurdles I will overcome:

◆
WEEKLY
Priorities

HIGH

MEDIUM

◆
DAILY
Habits

PRAYER
○ ○ ○ ○ ○ ○ ○

BIBLE
○ ○ ○ ○ ○ ○ ○

WATER
○ ○ ○ ○ ○ ○ ○

RECHARGE
○ ○ ○ ○ ○ ○ ○

○ ○ ○ ○ ○ ○ ○

○ ○ ○ ○ ○ ○ ○

○ ○ ○ ○ ○ ○ ○

○ ○ ○ ○ ○ ○ ○

MONDAY	TUESDAY	WEDNESDAY

This week I intend to:

I will focus on:

"Every weakness contains within itself a strength."
-SHŪSAKU ENDŌ

THURSDAY	FRIDAY	SATURDAY

SUNDAY

I am thankful for:

Hurdles I will overcome:

Looking
BACK

EVALUATING
THE
PAST MONTH

Physical Health	Work Goals	Relationship Goals
☆☆☆☆☆	☆☆☆☆☆	☆☆☆☆☆
Spiritual Growth	Family Time	Creativity
☆☆☆☆☆	☆☆☆☆☆	☆☆☆☆☆
Mental Health	Financial Goals	_____
☆☆☆☆☆	☆☆☆☆☆	☆☆☆☆☆

Would you give the areas above a 1-star review, a 5-star review, or something in between?

◆ WHAT WENT WELL THIS PAST MONTH ◆

_____

_____

_____

_____

_____

_____

_____

◆ WHAT DIDN'T GO WELL THIS PAST MONTH ◆

_____

_____

_____

_____

_____

_____

_____

MONTH _____

YEAR 20____

SUN	MON	TUES	WED	THURS	FRI	SAT

GETTING IT TOGETHER THIS MONTH

Family _____

_____

_____

Work Goals _____

_____

_____

Wellness Goals _____

_____

_____

Relationship Health _____

_____

_____

Financial Goals _____

_____

_____

Emotional Health _____

_____

_____

Spiritual Growth _____

_____

_____

Special Projects _____

_____

_____

How will I preserve my focus this month?

• MONTHLY *Budget Tracking* •

MONTHLY EXPENSES			MONTHLY INCOME		
Category	Amount	Date Paid	Category	Amount	Date Received
Rent/Mortgage			Monthly Income		
Utility 1			Additional Earnings		
Utility 2			Gifts		
Utility 3			Savings from Previous Month		
Cell Phone					
Car/Transportation					
Savings					
Credit Card 1					
Credit Card 2					
TOTAL BILLS			TOTAL INCOME		

NOTES

MEAL	MONDAY	TUESDAY	WEDNESDAY	THURSDAY	FRIDAY	SATURDAY	SUNDAY
Breakfast							
Lunch							
Dinner							

WEEK 1

MEAL	MONDAY	TUESDAY	WEDNESDAY	THURSDAY	FRIDAY	SATURDAY	SUNDAY
Breakfast							
Lunch							
Dinner							

WEEK 2

MEAL	MONDAY	TUESDAY	WEDNESDAY	THURSDAY	FRIDAY	SATURDAY	SUNDAY
Breakfast							
Lunch							
Dinner							

WEEK 3

MEAL	MONDAY	TUESDAY	WEDNESDAY	THURSDAY	FRIDAY	SATURDAY	SUNDAY
Breakfast							
Lunch							
Dinner							

WEEK 4

WEEKLY
Priorities

HIGH

MEDIUM

DAILY
Habits

PRAYER

○ ○ ○ ○ ○ ○ ○

BIBLE

○ ○ ○ ○ ○ ○ ○

WATER

○ ○ ○ ○ ○ ○ ○

RECHARGE

○ ○ ○ ○ ○ ○ ○

_____
○ ○ ○ ○ ○ ○ ○

_____
○ ○ ○ ○ ○ ○ ○

_____
○ ○ ○ ○ ○ ○ ○

_____
○ ○ ○ ○ ○ ○ ○

MONDAY	TUESDAY	WEDNESDAY

This week I intend to:

I will focus on:

THURSDAY	FRIDAY	SATURDAY

SUNDAY

am thankful for:

Hurdles I will overcome:

Get-
TO-DO
LIST

◆

WEEKLY

Priorities

HIGH

MEDIUM

◆

DAILY

Habits

PRAYER

○ ○ ○ ○ ○ ○ ○

BIBLE

○ ○ ○ ○ ○ ○ ○

WATER

○ ○ ○ ○ ○ ○ ○

RECHARGE

○ ○ ○ ○ ○ ○ ○

○ ○ ○ ○ ○ ○ ○

○ ○ ○ ○ ○ ○ ○

○ ○ ○ ○ ○ ○ ○

○ ○ ○ ○ ○ ○ ○

WEEK OF

_____

MONDAY	TUESDAY	WEDNESDAY

This week I intend to:

I will focus on:

"If you believe in a God who controls the big things, you have to believe in a God who controls the little things. It is we to whom things look 'little' or 'big.'" **–ELISABETH ELLIOT**

THURSDAY	FRIDAY	SATURDAY

SUNDAY

I am thankful for:

Hurdles I will overcome:

Get- TO-DO LIST

WEEKLY
Priorities

HIGH

MEDIUM

DAILY
Habits

PRAYER
○○○○○○○

BIBLE
○○○○○○○

WATER
○○○○○○○

RECHARGE
○○○○○○○

○○○○○○○

○○○○○○○

○○○○○○○

○○○○○○○

MONDAY	TUESDAY	WEDNESDAY

This week I intend to:

I will focus on:

"Whatever is true, whatever is honorable, whatever is pure, whatever is lovely, if there is anything worthy of praise, dwell on these things." –PHILIPPIANS 4:8 (NASB)

THURSDAY	FRIDAY	SATURDAY

SUNDAY

Get-
TO-DO
LIST

am thankful for:

Hurdles I will overcome:

◆

W E E K L Y

Priorities

HIGH

MEDIUM

MONDAY	TUESDAY	WEDNESDAY

◆

D A I L Y

Habits

PRAYER
○ ○ ○ ○ ○ ○ ○

BIBLE
○ ○ ○ ○ ○ ○ ○

WATER
○ ○ ○ ○ ○ ○ ○

RECHARGE
○ ○ ○ ○ ○ ○ ○

○ ○ ○ ○ ○ ○ ○

○ ○ ○ ○ ○ ○ ○

○ ○ ○ ○ ○ ○ ○

○ ○ ○ ○ ○ ○ ○

This week I intend to:

I will focus on:

"God does not give us everything we want, but He does fulfill His promises, leading us along the best and straightest paths to Himself." **–DIETRICH BONHOEFFER**

THURSDAY	FRIDAY	SATURDAY

SUNDAY

I am thankful for:

Hurdles I will overcome:

Get-
TO-DO
LIST

◆

WEEKLY

Priorities

HIGH

MEDIUM

◆

DAILY

Habits

PRAYER

○○○○○○○

BIBLE

○○○○○○○

WATER

○○○○○○○

RECHARGE

○○○○○○○

___

○○○○○○○

___

○○○○○○○

___

○○○○○○○

___

○○○○○○○

WEEK OF

_____

MONDAY	TUESDAY	WEDNESDAY

This week I intend to:

I will focus on:

"Fix your thoughts on Jesus, whom we acknowledge as our apostle and high priest." –HEBREWS 3:1

THURSDAY	FRIDAY	SATURDAY

SUNDAY

I am thankful for:

Hurdles I will overcome:

Get-
TO-DO
LIST

Looking BACK

EVALUATING THE PAST MONTH

Physical Health
☆ ☆ ☆ ☆ ☆

Work Goals
☆ ☆ ☆ ☆ ☆

Relationship Goals
☆ ☆ ☆ ☆ ☆

Spiritual Growth
☆ ☆ ☆ ☆ ☆

Family Time
☆ ☆ ☆ ☆ ☆

Creativity
☆ ☆ ☆ ☆ ☆

Mental Health
☆ ☆ ☆ ☆ ☆

Financial Goals
☆ ☆ ☆ ☆ ☆

_____
☆ ☆ ☆ ☆ ☆

Would you give the areas above a 1-star review, a 5-star review, or something in between?

◆ WHAT WENT WELL THIS PAST MONTH ◆

_____

_____

_____

_____

_____

_____

_____

◆ WHAT DIDN'T GO WELL THIS PAST MONTH ◆

_____

_____

_____

_____

_____

_____

_____

MONTH _____

YEAR **20** ____

SUN	MON	TUES	WED	THURS	FRI	SAT

GETTING IT TOGETHER THIS MONTH

Family _____

_____

_____

Work Goals _____

_____

_____

Wellness Goals _____

_____

_____

Relationship Health _____

_____

_____

Financial Goals _____

_____

_____

Emotional Health _____

_____

_____

Spiritual Growth _____

_____

_____

Special Projects _____

_____

_____

How will I be intentional this month?

MONTHLY *Budget Tracking*

MONTHLY EXPENSES			MONTHLY INCOME		
Category	Amount	Date Paid	Category	Amount	Date Received
Rent/Mortgage			Monthly Income		
Utility 1			Additional Earnings		
Utility 2			Gifts		
Utility 3			Savings from Previous Month		
Cell Phone					
Car/Transportation					
Savings					
Credit Card 1					
Credit Card 2					
TOTAL BILLS			TOTAL INCOME		

NOTES

MEAL	MONDAY	TUESDAY	WEDNESDAY	THURSDAY	FRIDAY	SATURDAY	SUNDAY
Breakfast							
Lunch							
Dinner							

WEEK 1

MEAL	MONDAY	TUESDAY	WEDNESDAY	THURSDAY	FRIDAY	SATURDAY	SUNDAY
Breakfast							
Lunch							
Dinner							

WEEK 2

MEAL	MONDAY	TUESDAY	WEDNESDAY	THURSDAY	FRIDAY	SATURDAY	SUNDAY
Breakfast							
Lunch							
Dinner							

WEEK 3

MEAL	MONDAY	TUESDAY	WEDNESDAY	THURSDAY	FRIDAY	SATURDAY	SUNDAY
Breakfast							
Lunch							
Dinner							

WEEK 4

◆

WEEKLY
Priorities

HIGH

MEDIUM

◆

DAILY
Habits

PRAYER
○ ○ ○ ○ ○ ○ ○

BIBLE
○ ○ ○ ○ ○ ○ ○

WATER
○ ○ ○ ○ ○ ○ ○

RECHARGE
○ ○ ○ ○ ○ ○ ○

○ ○ ○ ○ ○ ○ ○

○ ○ ○ ○ ○ ○ ○

○ ○ ○ ○ ○ ○ ○

○ ○ ○ ○ ○ ○ ○

WEEK OF
_____

MONDAY	TUESDAY	WEDNESDAY

This week I intend to:

I will focus on:

"Bridges are built not with passivity or avoidance but with the deep, hard work of seeking to understand."
–LATASHA MORRISON

THURSDAY	FRIDAY	SATURDAY

SUNDAY

Get-
TO-DO
LIST

I am thankful for:

Hurdles I will overcome:

_____

WEEKLY
Priorities

HIGH

MEDIUM

DAILY
Habits

PRAYER
◯ ◯ ◯ ◯ ◯ ◯ ◯

BIBLE
◯ ◯ ◯ ◯ ◯ ◯ ◯

WATER
◯ ◯ ◯ ◯ ◯ ◯ ◯

RECHARGE
◯ ◯ ◯ ◯ ◯ ◯ ◯

◯ ◯ ◯ ◯ ◯ ◯ ◯

◯ ◯ ◯ ◯ ◯ ◯ ◯

◯ ◯ ◯ ◯ ◯ ◯ ◯

◯ ◯ ◯ ◯ ◯ ◯ ◯

MONDAY	TUESDAY	WEDNESDAY

This week I intend to:

I will focus on:

"You will keep in perfect peace those whose minds are steadfast, because they trust in you." –ISAIAH 26:3

THURSDAY	FRIDAY	SATURDAY

SUNDAY

I am thankful for:

Hurdles I will overcome:

WEEKLY
Priorities
HIGH

MEDIUM

DAILY
Habits

PRAYER
◯ ◯ ◯ ◯ ◯ ◯ ◯

BIBLE
◯ ◯ ◯ ◯ ◯ ◯ ◯

WATER
◯ ◯ ◯ ◯ ◯ ◯ ◯

RECHARGE
◯ ◯ ◯ ◯ ◯ ◯ ◯

_____
◯ ◯ ◯ ◯ ◯ ◯ ◯

_____
◯ ◯ ◯ ◯ ◯ ◯ ◯

_____
◯ ◯ ◯ ◯ ◯ ◯ ◯

_____
◯ ◯ ◯ ◯ ◯ ◯ ◯

WEEK OF
_____

MONDAY	TUESDAY	WEDNESDAY

This week I intend to:

I will focus on:

"Our greatest fear should not be of failure but of succeeding at things in life that don't really matter." **–FRANCIS CHAN**

THURSDAY	FRIDAY	SATURDAY

SUNDAY

I am thankful for:

Hurdles I will overcome:

Get-
TO-DO
LIST

WEEKLY
Priorities
HIGH

MEDIUM

DAILY
Habits

PRAYER
○○○○○○○

BIBLE
○○○○○○○

WATER
○○○○○○○

RECHARGE
○○○○○○○

○○○○○○○

○○○○○○○

○○○○○○○

○○○○○○○

WEEK OF
_____

MONDAY	TUESDAY	WEDNESDAY

This week I intend to:

I will focus on:

"Neither death nor life, nor height nor depth, nor any other created thing, shall be able to separate us from the love of God." –ROMANS 8:38-39 (NKJV)

THURSDAY	FRIDAY	SATURDAY

SUNDAY

am thankful for:

Hurdles I will overcome:

WEEKLY
Priorities

HIGH

MEDIUM

DAILY
Habits

PRAYER
○ ○ ○ ○ ○ ○ ○

BIBLE
○ ○ ○ ○ ○ ○ ○

WATER
○ ○ ○ ○ ○ ○ ○

RECHARGE
○ ○ ○ ○ ○ ○ ○

○ ○ ○ ○ ○ ○ ○

○ ○ ○ ○ ○ ○ ○

○ ○ ○ ○ ○ ○ ○

○ ○ ○ ○ ○ ○ ○

MONDAY	TUESDAY	WEDNESDAY

This week I intend to:

I will focus on:

We are all faced with a series of great opportunities rilliantly disguised as impossible situations."

CHUCK SWINDOLL

Get-TO-DO LIST

THURSDAY	FRIDAY	SATURDAY

SUNDAY

am thankful for:

urdles I will overcome:

Looking BACK

EVALUATING THE PAST MONTH

Physical Health
☆☆☆☆☆

Work Goals
☆☆☆☆☆

Relationship Goals
☆☆☆☆☆

Spiritual Growth
☆☆☆☆☆

Family Time
☆☆☆☆☆

Creativity
☆☆☆☆☆

Mental Health
☆☆☆☆☆

Financial Goals
☆☆☆☆☆

_____
☆☆☆☆☆

Would you give the areas above a 1-star review, a 5-star review, or something in between?

◆ WHAT WENT WELL THIS PAST MONTH ◆

_____
_____
_____
_____
_____
_____
_____
_____

◆ WHAT DIDN'T GO WELL THIS PAST MONTH ◆

_____
_____
_____
_____
_____
_____
_____

MONTH _____

YEAR 20 ____

SUN	MON	TUES	WED	THURS	FRI	SAT

GETTING IT TOGETHER THIS MONTH

Family _____

Work Goals _____

Wellness Goals _____

Relationship Health _____

Financial Goals _____

Emotional Health _____

Spiritual Growth _____

Special Projects _____

How will I realign my priorities this month?

MONTHLY *Budget Tracking*

MONTHLY EXPENSES			MONTHLY INCOME		
Category	Amount	Date Paid	Category	Amount	Date Received
Rent/Mortgage			Monthly Income		
Utility 1			Additional Earnings		
Utility 2			Gifts		
Utility 3			Savings from Previous Month		
Cell Phone					
Car/Transportation					
Savings					
Credit Card 1					
Credit Card 2					
TOTAL BILLS			TOTAL INCOME		

NOTES _____

_____

_____

_____

_____

MONTHLY *Menu Planner*

MONTH 10

MEAL	MONDAY	TUESDAY	WEDNESDAY	THURSDAY	FRIDAY	SATURDAY	SUNDAY
Breakfast							
Lunch							
Dinner							

WEEK 1

MEAL	MONDAY	TUESDAY	WEDNESDAY	THURSDAY	FRIDAY	SATURDAY	SUNDAY
Breakfast							
Lunch							
Dinner							

WEEK 2

MEAL	MONDAY	TUESDAY	WEDNESDAY	THURSDAY	FRIDAY	SATURDAY	SUNDAY
Breakfast							
Lunch							
Dinner							

WEEK 3

MEAL	MONDAY	TUESDAY	WEDNESDAY	THURSDAY	FRIDAY	SATURDAY	SUNDAY
Breakfast							
Lunch							
Dinner							

WEEK 4

◆

WEEKLY

Priorities

HIGH

MEDIUM

◆

DAILY

Habits

PRAYER
◯◯◯◯◯◯◯

BIBLE
◯◯◯◯◯◯◯

WATER
◯◯◯◯◯◯◯

RECHARGE
◯◯◯◯◯◯◯

◯◯◯◯◯◯◯

◯◯◯◯◯◯◯

◯◯◯◯◯◯◯

◯◯◯◯◯◯◯

MONDAY	TUESDAY	WEDNESDAY

This week I intend to:

I will focus on:

"The Lord is my rock, my fortress and my deliverer; my God is my rock, in whom I take refuge, my shield and the horn of my salvation, my stronghold." – PSALM 18:2

THURSDAY	FRIDAY	SATURDAY

SUNDAY

I am thankful for:

Hurdles I will overcome:

Get-TO-DO LIST

◆

WEEKLY

Priorities

HIGH

MEDIUM

◆

DAILY

Habits

PRAYER
○ ○ ○ ○ ○ ○ ○

BIBLE
○ ○ ○ ○ ○ ○ ○

WATER
○ ○ ○ ○ ○ ○ ○

RECHARGE
○ ○ ○ ○ ○ ○ ○

○ ○ ○ ○ ○ ○ ○

○ ○ ○ ○ ○ ○ ○

○ ○ ○ ○ ○ ○ ○

○ ○ ○ ○ ○ ○ ○

WEEK OF

_____

MONDAY	TUESDAY	WEDNESDAY

This week I intend to:

I will focus on:

"Let God's promises shine on your problems."
CORRIE TEN BOOM

THURSDAY	FRIDAY	SATURDAY

SUNDAY

am thankful for:

Hurdles I will overcome:

◆

W E E K L Y

Priorities

HIGH

MEDIUM

◆

D A I L Y

Habits

PRAYER

○ ○ ○ ○ ○ ○ ○

BIBLE

○ ○ ○ ○ ○ ○ ○

WATER

○ ○ ○ ○ ○ ○ ○

RECHARGE

○ ○ ○ ○ ○ ○ ○

○ ○ ○ ○ ○ ○ ○

○ ○ ○ ○ ○ ○ ○

○ ○ ○ ○ ○ ○ ○

○ ○ ○ ○ ○ ○ ○

MONDAY	TUESDAY	WEDNESDAY

This week I intend to:

I will focus on:

"May the God of hope fill you with all joy and peace in believing, so that by the power of the Holy Spirit you may abound in hope." –ROMANS 15:13 (ESV)

THURSDAY	FRIDAY	SATURDAY

SUNDAY

am thankful for:

Hurdles I will overcome:

Get— TO-DO LIST

◆

WEEKLY
Priorities

HIGH

MEDIUM

◆

DAILY
Habits

PRAYER
○○○○○○○

BIBLE
○○○○○○○

WATER
○○○○○○○

RECHARGE
○○○○○○○

○○○○○○○

○○○○○○○

○○○○○○○

○○○○○○○

WEEK OF

_____

MONDAY	TUESDAY	WEDNESDAY

This week I intend to:

I will focus on:

"Sometimes you need to feel the pain and sting of defeat to activate the real passion and purpose that God predestined inside of you." –CHADWICK BOSEMAN

Get-
TO-DO
LIST

THURSDAY	FRIDAY	SATURDAY

SUNDAY

I am thankful for:

Hurdles I will overcome:

◆

_____

MONDAY	TUESDAY	WEDNESDAY

◆

WEEKLY

Priorities

HIGH

MEDIUM

◆

DAILY

Habits

PRAYER

○ ○ ○ ○ ○ ○ ○

BIBLE

○ ○ ○ ○ ○ ○ ○

WATER

○ ○ ○ ○ ○ ○ ○

RECHARGE

○ ○ ○ ○ ○ ○ ○

_____
○ ○ ○ ○ ○ ○ ○

_____
○ ○ ○ ○ ○ ○ ○

_____
○ ○ ○ ○ ○ ○ ○

_____
○ ○ ○ ○ ○ ○ ○

This week I intend to:

I will focus on:

"I have said these things to you, that in me you may have peace. In the world you will have tribulation. But take heart; I have overcome the world." –JOHN 16:33 (ESV)

THURSDAY	FRIDAY	SATURDAY
		SUNDAY

I am thankful for:

Hurdles I will overcome:

Get-TO-DO LIST

Looking BACK

EVALUATING
THE
PAST MONTH

Physical Health
☆ ☆ ☆ ☆ ☆

Work Goals
☆ ☆ ☆ ☆ ☆

Relationship Goals
☆ ☆ ☆ ☆ ☆

Spiritual Growth
☆ ☆ ☆ ☆ ☆

Family Time
☆ ☆ ☆ ☆ ☆

Creativity
☆ ☆ ☆ ☆ ☆

Mental Health
☆ ☆ ☆ ☆ ☆

Financial Goals
☆ ☆ ☆ ☆ ☆

_____
☆ ☆ ☆ ☆ ☆

Would you give the areas above a 1-star review, a 5-star review, or something in between?

◆ WHAT WENT WELL THIS PAST MONTH ◆

◆ WHAT DIDN'T GO WELL THIS PAST MONTH ◆

MONTH _____

YEAR 20 ____

SUN	MON	TUES	WED	THURS	FRI	SAT

GETTING IT TOGETHER THIS MONTH

Family _____

Work Goals _____

Wellness Goals _____

Relationship Health _____

Financial Goals _____

Emotional Health _____

Spiritual Growth _____

Special Projects _____

How will I renew my spirit this month?

• MONTHLY *Budget Tracking* •

MONTHLY EXPENSES			MONTHLY INCOME		
Category	Amount	Date Paid	Category	Amount	Date Received
Rent/Mortgage			Monthly Income		
Utility 1			Additional Earnings		
Utility 2			Gifts		
Utility 3			Savings from Previous Month		
Cell Phone					
Car/Transportation					
Savings					
Credit Card 1					
Credit Card 2					
TOTAL BILLS			TOTAL INCOME		

NOTES

MEAL	MONDAY	TUESDAY	WEDNESDAY	THURSDAY	FRIDAY	SATURDAY	SUNDAY
Breakfast							
Lunch							
Dinner							

WEEK 1

MEAL	MONDAY	TUESDAY	WEDNESDAY	THURSDAY	FRIDAY	SATURDAY	SUNDAY
Breakfast							
Lunch							
Dinner							

WEEK 2

MEAL	MONDAY	TUESDAY	WEDNESDAY	THURSDAY	FRIDAY	SATURDAY	SUNDAY
Breakfast							
Lunch							
Dinner							

WEEK 3

MEAL	MONDAY	TUESDAY	WEDNESDAY	THURSDAY	FRIDAY	SATURDAY	SUNDAY
Breakfast							
Lunch							
Dinner							

WEEK 4

◆

WEEKLY
Priorities

HIGH

MEDIUM

MONDAY	TUESDAY	WEDNESDAY

◆

DAILY
Habits

PRAYER
○○○○○○○

BIBLE
○○○○○○○

WATER
○○○○○○○

RECHARGE
○○○○○○○

○○○○○○○

○○○○○○○

○○○○○○○

○○○○○○○

This week I intend to:

I will focus on:

"Relying on God has to start all over every day, as if nothing has yet been done." –C. S. LEWIS

THURSDAY	FRIDAY	SATURDAY

SUNDAY

I am thankful for:

Hurdles I will overcome:

◆

W E E K L Y
Priorities

HIGH

MEDIUM

◆

D A I L Y
Habits

PRAYER
○ ○ ○ ○ ○ ○ ○

BIBLE
○ ○ ○ ○ ○ ○ ○

WATER
○ ○ ○ ○ ○ ○ ○

RECHARGE
○ ○ ○ ○ ○ ○ ○

_____
○ ○ ○ ○ ○ ○ ○

_____
○ ○ ○ ○ ○ ○ ○

_____
○ ○ ○ ○ ○ ○ ○

_____
○ ○ ○ ○ ○ ○ ○

MONDAY	TUESDAY	WEDNESDAY

This week I intend to:

I will focus on:

"Those who hope in the Lord will renew their strength. They will soar on wings like eagles; they will run and not grow weary, they will walk and not be faint." —ISAIAH 40:31

THURSDAY	FRIDAY	SATURDAY

SUNDAY

I am thankful for:

Hurdles I will overcome:

◆

WEEKLY

Priorities

HIGH

MEDIUM

◆

DAILY

Habits

PRAYER

○○○○○○○

BIBLE

○○○○○○○

WATER

○○○○○○○

RECHARGE

○○○○○○○

_____

○○○○○○○

_____

○○○○○○○

_____

○○○○○○○

_____

○○○○○○○

MONDAY	TUESDAY	WEDNESDAY

This week I intend to:

I will focus on:

"It is okay if you find yourself a little more fragile than usual. Be gentle with your well-being. Tread softly with your soul."

—ARIELLE ESTORIA

THURSDAY	FRIDAY	SATURDAY

SUNDAY

I am thankful for:

Hurdles I will overcome:

Get-TO-DO LIST

WEEKLY
Priorities

HIGH

MEDIUM

DAILY
Habits

PRAYER
○ ○ ○ ○ ○ ○ ○

BIBLE
○ ○ ○ ○ ○ ○ ○

WATER
○ ○ ○ ○ ○ ○ ○

RECHARGE
○ ○ ○ ○ ○ ○ ○

○ ○ ○ ○ ○ ○ ○

○ ○ ○ ○ ○ ○ ○

○ ○ ○ ○ ○ ○ ○

○ ○ ○ ○ ○ ○ ○

MONDAY	TUESDAY	WEDNESDAY

This week I intend to:

I will focus on:

"Do not conform to the pattern of this world, but be transformed by the renewing of your mind. Then you will be able to test and approve what God's will is." –ROMANS 12:2

THURSDAY	FRIDAY	SATURDAY

SUNDAY

I am thankful for:

Hurdles I will overcome:

◆

WEEKLY

Priorities

HIGH

MEDIUM

◆

DAILY

Habits

PRAYER
○ ○ ○ ○ ○ ○ ○

BIBLE
○ ○ ○ ○ ○ ○ ○

WATER
○ ○ ○ ○ ○ ○ ○

RECHARGE
○ ○ ○ ○ ○ ○ ○

_____
○ ○ ○ ○ ○ ○ ○

_____
○ ○ ○ ○ ○ ○ ○

_____
○ ○ ○ ○ ○ ○ ○

_____
○ ○ ○ ○ ○ ○ ○

WEEK OF

_____

MONDAY	TUESDAY	WEDNESDAY

This week I intend to:

I will focus on:

"God is able to take the mess of our past and turn it into a message. He takes the trials and tests and turns them into a testimony." –CHRISTINE CAINE

THURSDAY	FRIDAY	SATURDAY

SUNDAY

Get-
TO-DO
LIST

am thankful for:

Hurdles I will overcome:

Looking BACK

EVALUATING THE PAST MONTH

Physical Health
☆☆☆☆☆

Work Goals
☆☆☆☆☆

Relationship Goals
☆☆☆☆☆

Spiritual Growth
☆☆☆☆☆

Family Time
☆☆☆☆☆

Creativity
☆☆☆☆☆

Mental Health
☆☆☆☆☆

Financial Goals
☆☆☆☆☆

_____
☆☆☆☆☆

Would you give the areas above a 1-star review, a 5-star review, or something in between?

◆ WHAT WENT WELL THIS PAST MONTH ◆

◆ WHAT DIDN'T GO WELL THIS PAST MONTH ◆

MONTH _____

YEAR 20 ____

SUN	MON	TUES	WED	THURS	FRI	SAT

GETTING IT TOGETHER THIS MONTH

Family _____

Work Goals _____

Wellness Goals _____

Relationship Health _____

Financial Goals _____

Emotional Health _____

Spiritual Growth _____

Special Projects _____

Where can I discover wonder this month?

• MONTHLY *Budget Tracking* •

MONTHLY EXPENSES			MONTHLY INCOME		
Category	Amount	Date Paid	Category	Amount	Date Received
Rent/Mortgage			Monthly Income		
Utility 1			Additional Earnings		
Utility 2			Gifts		
Utility 3			Savings from Previous Month		
Cell Phone					
Car/Transportation					
Savings					
Credit Card 1					
Credit Card 2					
TOTAL BILLS			TOTAL INCOME		

NOTES _____

_____

_____

_____

_____

MEAL	MONDAY	TUESDAY	WEDNESDAY	THURSDAY	FRIDAY	SATURDAY	SUNDAY
Breakfast							
Lunch							
Dinner							

WEEK 1

Breakfast							
Lunch							
Dinner							

WEEK 2

Breakfast							
Lunch							
Dinner							

WEEK 3

Breakfast							
Lunch							
Dinner							

WEEK 4

WEEKLY
Priorities
HIGH

MEDIUM

DAILY
Habits

PRAYER
○ ○ ○ ○ ○ ○ ○

BIBLE
○ ○ ○ ○ ○ ○ ○

WATER
○ ○ ○ ○ ○ ○ ○

RECHARGE
○ ○ ○ ○ ○ ○ ○

_____
○ ○ ○ ○ ○ ○ ○

_____
○ ○ ○ ○ ○ ○ ○

_____
○ ○ ○ ○ ○ ○ ○

_____
○ ○ ○ ○ ○ ○ ○

WEEK OF
_____

MONDAY	TUESDAY	WEDNESDAY

This week I intend to:

I will focus on:

"The will of God will not take us where the grace of God cannot sustain us." **–BILLY GRAHAM**

Get-
TO-DO
LIST

THURSDAY	FRIDAY	SATURDAY
		SUNDAY

I am thankful for:

Hurdles I will overcome:

◆

W E E K L Y

Priorities

HIGH

MEDIUM

◆

D A I L Y

Habits

PRAYER

○ ○ ○ ○ ○ ○ ○

BIBLE

○ ○ ○ ○ ○ ○ ○

WATER

○ ○ ○ ○ ○ ○ ○

RECHARGE

○ ○ ○ ○ ○ ○ ○

○ ○ ○ ○ ○ ○ ○

○ ○ ○ ○ ○ ○ ○

○ ○ ○ ○ ○ ○ ○

○ ○ ○ ○ ○ ○ ○

WEEK OF

_____

MONDAY	TUESDAY	WEDNESDAY

This week I intend to:

I will focus on:

"So do not fear, for I am with you; do not be dismayed, for I am your God. I will strengthen you and help you."
–ISAIAH 41:10 (ESV)

THURSDAY	FRIDAY	SATURDAY

SUNDAY

I am thankful for:

Hurdles I will overcome:

◆

WEEKLY

Priorities

HIGH

MEDIUM

◆

DAILY

Habits

PRAYER

○○○○○○○

BIBLE

○○○○○○○

WATER

○○○○○○○

RECHARGE

○○○○○○○

○○○○○○○

○○○○○○○

○○○○○○○

○○○○○○○

WEEK OF

_____

MONDAY	TUESDAY	WEDNESDAY

This week I intend to:

I will focus on:

"Shalom is not a utopian destination; it is a constant journey." **-RANDY WOODLEY**

THURSDAY	FRIDAY	SATURDAY

SUNDAY

I am thankful for:

Hurdles I will overcome:

◆

MEDIUM

◆

DAILY

Habits

PRAYER

◯◯◯◯◯◯◯

BIBLE

◯◯◯◯◯◯◯

WATER

◯◯◯◯◯◯◯

RECHARGE

◯◯◯◯◯◯◯

◯◯◯◯◯◯◯

◯◯◯◯◯◯◯

◯◯◯◯◯◯◯

◯◯◯◯◯◯◯

WEEK OF

MONDAY	TUESDAY	WEDNESDAY

This week I intend to:

I will focus on:

"God is our refuge and strength, a very present help in trouble." –PSALM 46:1 (KJV)

THURSDAY	FRIDAY	SATURDAY

SUNDAY

I am thankful for:

Hurdles I will overcome:

WEEKLY

Priorities

HIGH

MEDIUM

DAILY

Habits

PRAYER

○ ○ ○ ○ ○ ○ ○

BIBLE

○ ○ ○ ○ ○ ○ ○

WATER

○ ○ ○ ○ ○ ○ ○

RECHARGE

○ ○ ○ ○ ○ ○ ○

○ ○ ○ ○ ○ ○ ○

○ ○ ○ ○ ○ ○ ○

○ ○ ○ ○ ○ ○ ○

○ ○ ○ ○ ○ ○ ○

WEEK OF

_____

MONDAY	TUESDAY	WEDNESDAY

This week I intend to:

I will focus on:

"Keep on beginning and failing. Each time you fail, start all over again, and you will grow stronger until you have accomplished a purpose." **–ANNE SULLIVAN**

THURSDAY	FRIDAY	SATURDAY

SUNDAY

I am thankful for:

Hurdles I will overcome:

Get-TO-DO LIST

EVALUATING THE PAST YEAR

Physical Health
☆☆☆☆☆

Work Goals
☆☆☆☆☆

Relationship Goals
☆☆☆☆☆

Spiritual Growth
☆☆☆☆☆

Family Time
☆☆☆☆☆

Creativity
☆☆☆☆☆

Mental Health
☆☆☆☆☆

Financial Goals
☆☆☆☆☆

☆☆☆☆☆

Would you give the areas above a 1-star review, a 5-star review, or something in between?

◆ HOW I GOT IT TOGETHER THIS YEAR ◆

◆ WHAT I'D LIKE TO BUILD ON IN THE YEAR AHEAD ◆

Things to Get Together

- [ ]
- [ ]
- [ ]
- [ ]
- [ ]
- [ ]
- [ ]
- [ ]
- [ ]
- [ ]
- [ ]
- [ ]
- [ ]
- [ ]
- [ ]
- [ ]
- [ ]
- [ ]
- [ ]
- [ ]
- [ ]
- [ ]

Things to Remember

Things to Get Together

- [ ] _____
- [ ] _____
- [ ] _____
- [ ] _____
- [ ] _____
- [ ] _____
- [ ] _____
- [ ] _____
- [ ] _____
- [ ] _____
- [ ] _____
- [ ] _____
- [ ] _____
- [ ] _____
- [ ] _____
- [ ] _____
- [ ] _____
- [ ] _____
- [ ] _____
- [ ] _____
- [ ] _____
- [ ] _____

Things to Remember

Things to Get Together

Things to Remember

JANUARY

FEBRUARY

MARCH

APRIL

MAY

JUNE

JULY

AUGUST

SEPTEMBER

OCTOBER

NOVEMBER

DECEMBER

Endurance

Consistency

Vacation!

MENTAL HEALTH DAY

Reminder

Reminder

Birthday

Birthday

Celebrate

Appointment

Appointment

Appointment

Decisiveness

Discipline

Breathe

Intentionality

• WONDER •

• FOCUS •

• RENEW •

• REALIGN •

Alive

Dare
TO
dream

TO
DO

TO
DO

TO
DO

DAY
OFF

DAY
OFF

◆ ACKNOWLEDGMENTS ◆

Thank you to all of the individuals and departments within the
Random House Division and WaterBrook for their help in creating
this project. In particular, thank you to the following people:

PORSCHA BURKE

SUSAN TJADEN

NICOLE BLOCK

LESLIE CALHOUN

DANIELLE DESCHENES

LUISA FRANCAVILLA

DEREK GULLINO

JESSIE KAYE

JAMIE LAPEYROLERIE

PHILIP LEUNG

MARK McCAUSLIN

LAURA PALESE

MARYSARAH QUINN

CHRISTINE TANIGAWA

KIM VON FANGE

ERICKA WEED

CHELSEA WOODWARD